Hear Your HEART

by Paul Showers • illustrated by Holly Keller

HarperCollinsPublishers

For Marie-Laure, with thanks
—H.K.

With special thanks to Richard A. Manzi, M.D., for his time and expert review

The Let's-Read-and-Find-Out Science book series was originated by Dr. Franklyn M. Branley, Astronomer Emeritus and former Chairman of the American Museum–Hayden Planetarium, and was formerly co-edited by him and Dr. Roma Gans, Professor Emeritus of Childhood Education, Teachers College, Columbia University. Text and illustrations for each of the books in the series are checked for accuracy by an expert in the relevant field. For more information about Let's-Read-and-Find-Out Science books, write to HarperCollins Children's Books, 1350 Avenue of the Americas, New York, NY 10019, or visit our web site at www.letsreadandfindout.com.

Library of Congress Cataloging-in-Publication Data
Showers, Paul.
   Hear your heart / by Paul Showers; illustrated by Holly Keller.
      p.   cm.—(Let's-read-and-find-out science. Stage 2)
   Summary: A simple explanation of the structure of the heart and how it works.
   ISBN 0-06-025410-6.—ISBN 0-06-025411-4 (lib. bdg.).—ISBN 0-06-445139-9 (pbk.)
   1. Heart—Juvenile literature.   [1. Heart.]   I. Keller, Holly, ill.   II. Title.   III. Series.
QP111.6.S48   2001   99-41336
612.1'7—dc21   CIP

Typography by Elynn Cohen   1   2   3   4   5   6   7   8   9   10   ❖   Revised and Newly Illustrated Edition

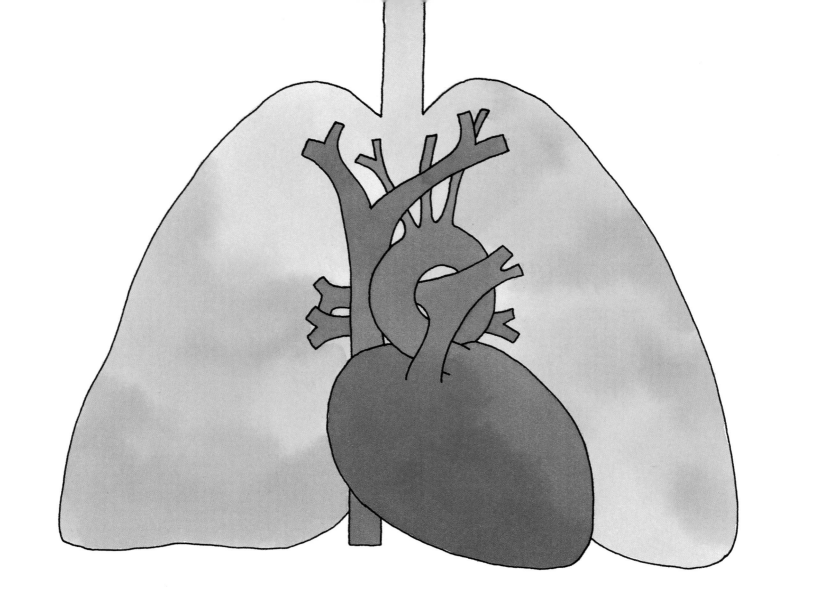

Hear Your Heart

When I visit the doctor, he listens to my heart
with a stethoscope.

The stethoscope is cold. It makes me shiver.

I like my stethoscope much better. It isn't cold.

My stethoscope is a cardboard tube.

My sister, Lisa, has one, too.

We save tubes and turn them into stethoscopes.

Sometimes they are tubes from old rolls of paper towels.

Sometimes they are tubes from old toilet-paper rolls. Any kind of cardboard tube will do.

This is how you listen to someone's heart:

Ask a friend to find the heartbeat on the left side of her chest.

Put one end of your tube on this spot.

Now put your ear at the other end.

We listen to our friends' hearts, and they listen to ours.

Phil's heart beats like this: *pum-PUM pum-PUM*
pum-PUM pum-PUM.

Molly's heart beats the same way.

So does mine. So does Lisa's.

Dad's heart is a little slower. It beats like this:
ka-DUM ka-DUM ka-DUM ka-DUM.

Andrew is only eleven months old.

Mom holds him so we can listen to his heart.

Andrew's heart has a very quick beat. It goes:

tup-pa tup-pa tup-pa tup-pa tup-pa.

Put your hand on your chest.
Can you feel your heart?

Your heart is about as big as
your fist.

It doesn't look like a heart
on a valentine.

It is shaped more like a pear.

Your heart has tubes attached
to it.

When your heart beats, it moves
blood through your body.

Your heart is full of blood.

When it beats, it squeezes itself together.

That's when the heart contracts.

Blood squirts out into some of the tubes.

Then your heart stops squeezing and opens up again.

That's when the heart expands.

Blood flows into it through the other tubes.

Blood flows away from your heart in tubes called arteries.

Blood flows into your heart in tubes called veins.

In this picture the arteries are colored red.

The veins are black.

Your heart is a strong muscle.
Night and day it squeezes
opens
squeezes
opens.
It is always beating.

A heart is divided into two halves.

Each half has several veins and one artery attached to it.

Each half has two little doors in it.

These doors are called valves.

In this drawing the valves to the arteries are colored red.

The valves from the veins are black.

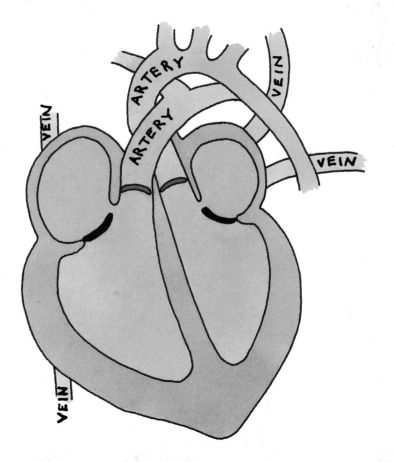

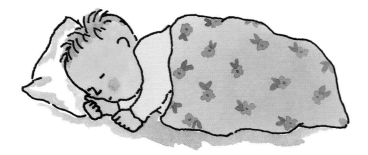

All day long, all night long, these valves open and close, open and close.

When the black valves open, the red valves close.

When the red valves open, the black valves close.

The valves keep the blood moving in the right direction—IN from the veins, OUT through the arteries.

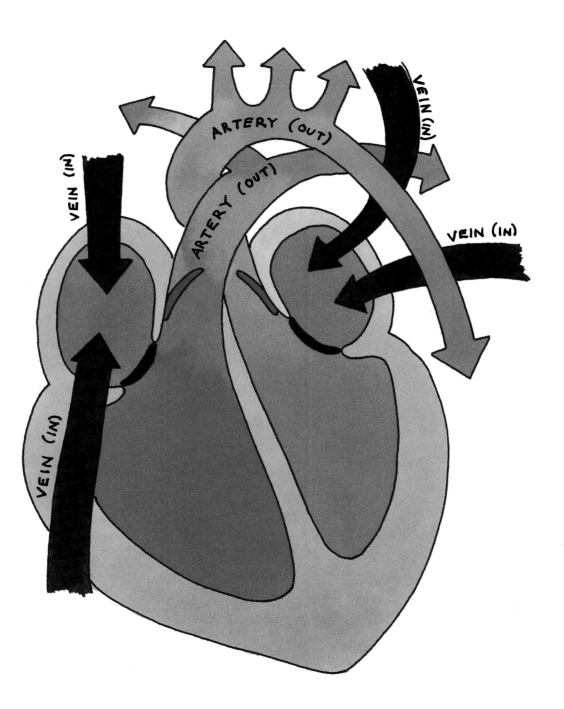

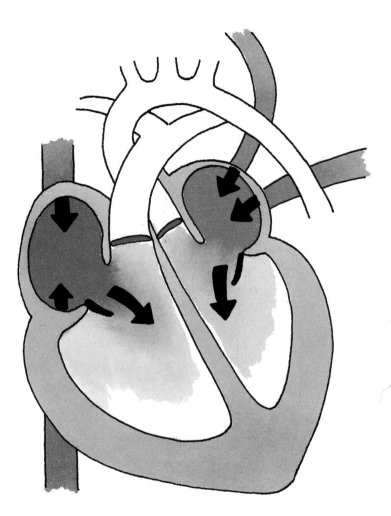

When a heart beats, each half works the same way.

First, blood comes in from the big veins at the top of the heart.

The black valves are open. Blood flows into the heart.

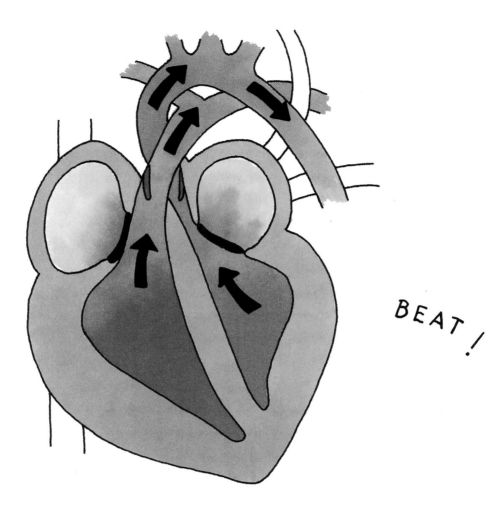

BEAT !

Then the heart contracts and pushes the blood.
The black valves close. The red valves open.
Blood cannot flow back into the veins.
It can only flow out through the arteries.

Big arteries spread out from your heart.

They go to your arms and legs and head.

Smaller arteries branch out from the big ones.

They branch out to the top of your head to the tips of your fingers

to the tips of your toes

to every part of your body.

When blood reaches the very smallest arteries, it passes into tiny veins.

The tiny veins run into bigger and bigger veins that carry the blood back to the heart.

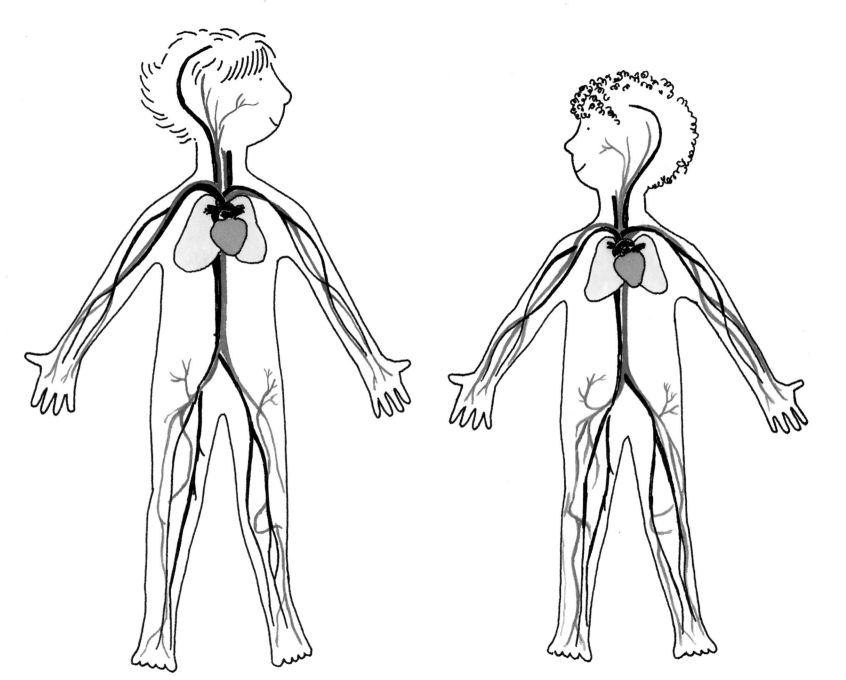

BEAT-PUSH BEAT-PUSH

Touch your wrist just below your thumb.

Press gently with your fingertips.

Do you feel something push against your fingers? *push push push*.

You are feeling a small artery in your wrist.

Your heart is pushing blood through it: *beat—push beat—push beat—push*.

This is your pulse.

You can only feel your pulse in an artery.

You can see your veins, but you cannot feel a pulse in them.

Your pulse tells you how fast your heart is beating.
How fast is your heart beating right now as you read this book?
Get a watch with a second hand and count your pulse.
How many times does your heart beat in one minute?

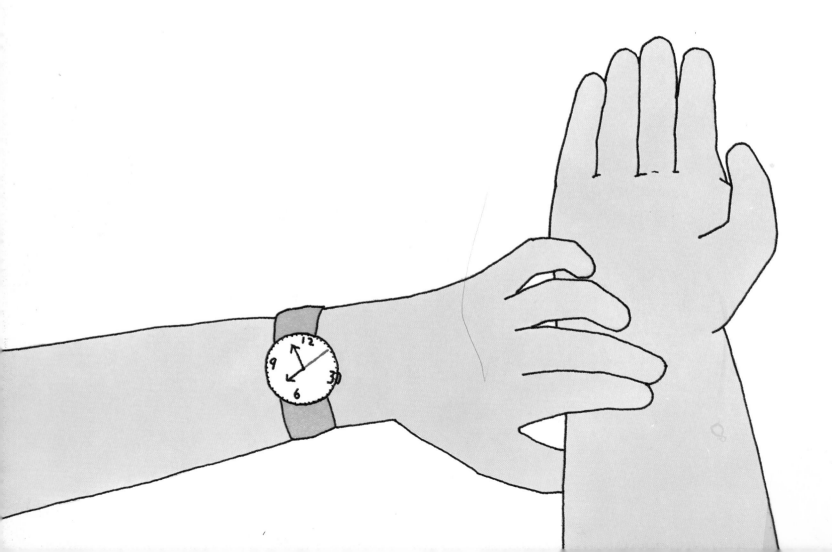

A man's heart beats about 72 times a minute: *ka-DUM*
ka-DUM ka-DUM ka-DUM ka-DUM.

An eight-year-old's heart beats about 90 times a
minute: *pum-PUM pum-PUM pum-PUM pum-PUM*.

A baby's heart beats more than 120 times a
minute: *tup-pa tup-pa tup-pa tup-pa tup-pa*.

Sometimes it goes a little faster, sometimes a little slower.

Your heart beats faster when you exercise.
Try this and see for yourself.
Hop up and down on one foot twenty times.
Now feel your pulse.
Use your watch to count your pulse.
How fast is your heart beating now?

Your heart beats faster when you run or jump.
When you sleep, it beats much slower.

A big animal's heart beats more slowly than a little animal's.
An elephant's heart beats only 20 to 25 times a minute.

A mouse's heart beats
more than 500 times a minute.

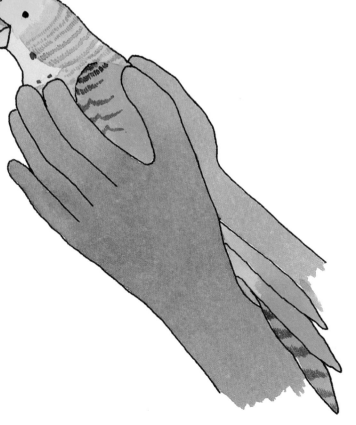

Lisa has a parakeet named Clarence.
When we hold him gently, we can feel his
heart beating: *Pat-pat-pat-pat-pat.*
It beats so fast, we can't keep count.

Your heart works all the time.

No other part of your body works as hard.

Your hand is strong, but not as strong as your heart.
Try this:

Open your hand. Close it in a fist. Open it. Close it.

How long before your hand gets tired?

Your heart never gets tired.

When you are awake

when you are asleep

your heart keeps moving blood through your body.

31

- ## How to Measure Your Heart Rate

1. Hold out the middle and index fingers of one hand together.
2. Place them on your other wrist at the base of the thumb until you feel a soft beating. You may have to try a few different spots until you find the right one.
3. Have a friend time you as you count the number of beats for one minute. This is your resting heart rate.

- ## How to Exercise Your Heart

You and a friend can try something fun to exercise your heart:

Invent a new dance to your favorite song.
Count how many jumping jacks you can do in one minute.
Play a game of tag.
Go roller-skating.
Play catch.

Do one or a couple of these activities for twenty minutes. When you are finished, count your heart rate again. Your heart rate will be higher (there will be more beats per minute). This is because exercising makes your heart beat faster, helping it stay healthy and strong. It is important to exercise a few times each week for at least twenty minutes. Not only will it keep your heart strong, it will keep your body strong as well.

How to Make a Stethoscope

You don't have to be a doctor to hear someone's heartbeat. You can make your own stethoscope at home.

You will need:

> 1 cardboard tube from an empty paper-towel roll
> 1 friend

1. Your friend can find his or her heart by placing one hand flat on the left side of his or her chest and feeling for the beat.
2. Place one end of the tube on the spot where your friend felt his or her heartbeat.
3. Put your ear at the other end of the tube, and you will hear your friend's quiet heartbeat.
4. Let your friend have a turn listening to your heart.

Web Site

Visit this web site to find out more about your heart and how you can keep it healthy: http://www.americanheart.org/Health/Lifestyle/Youth.

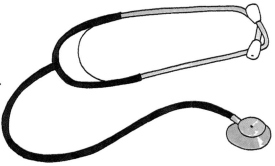